# In the Garden

A COLLECTION OF GARDENING ARTICLES

AND

BLANK JOURNAL PAGES

HEIDI SKINNER

Copyright © 2019 Heidi Skinner

All rights reserved.

No part of this book may be reproduced in any form or by any electronic or mechanical means, including information storage and retrieval systems, without written permission from the author.

*For all my friends and family who like to garden*

Articles in this journal are reprints, previously published in The Newport Voice, **2005** edition.

As such, please note the weather conditions and festival dates are incorrect for the current year.

# January

The start of a new year brings with it a new gardening season. Gardening has been taking a catnap and now it's beginning to awaken, slowly, yawning and stretching. Although it seems too early to even be thinking about starting a garden, the end of January is a perfect time to start planting cool season crops such as cabbage, potatoes, peas, onions, and broccoli. Besides the fact theses plants love cool weather, the insects are almost non-existent this early.

Just a reminder, send your soil samples in early, before the Agronomics Department gets busy.* Sample boxes and instructions can be picked up at local garden centers or at the Carteret County Agriculture Extension office. The testing is free except for the cost of the postage. This is the best way to determine how much lime and fertilizer you need for a great garden or lawn. The results can be hard to decipher so don't be shy about asking for help!

When, and if, we ever get a cold snap that lasts for more than two days, grape vines need to be pruned. Late January or into February is a good time. Grape vines need to be dormant when pruned so they don't "bleed" to death. For specific pruning instructions, you can check with the Agricultural Extension office. They have great horticultural leaflets on almost any gardening subject. Your local library is also a great source of information.

Winter blahs getting you down? Try forcing a few forsythia branches into bloom! Cut branches with lots of buds and put them in a vase or jar with a couple inches of water, making sure to trim off any buds that will be under water. Place branches in a dark or dim room for a couple of days. Take them out, change the water, and in a couple days to a week or so, you should have bright yellow blooms to cheer you up! This can be done with other flowering shrubs as well. Have fun experimenting! The closer the shrubs are to regular bloom time the less time it takes to force them. Sometimes, the branches will even root and you will have more shrubs to plant or share!

Until it's really warm enough to garden in earnest, relax! Kick back in your favorite chair with a cup of cocoa, hot tea, or coffee and enjoy perusing all the great seed catalogs that will soon be filling our mailboxes. Don't get too upset if your garden doesn't look just like those pictures in the catalogs. The difference between those pictures and your garden is like the difference between the honeymoon and the marriage! Besides, if you can garden successfully in eastern North Carolina with the heat, humidity, and insects, you can garden anywhere!

*This is outdated information. The Ag Extension now charges $4. per sample if you send them in after Thanksgiving and before the first of April. To avoid peak season, check your dates and get your samples in April through late November at no cost to you except postage.

# JANUARY

SEEDS

PLANTS

REMINDERS AND TO DO LIST

# JANUARY

### FERTILIZER & LIME

### PLANTING DATES

### WEATHER

### INSECTS

### HARVEST DATES

# JANUARY

WHAT I PLANTED WHERE

# February

If February was an hour, it would be the hour before dawn. The darkest, coldest, most dismal, seems like it's never going to end hour. So it is in the gardening world. It seems like February will never end and it will never warm up enough for things to green up and start growing again. February ushers in spring, like the first hint of light limns the edge of the world and heralds the arrival of the sun.

Daffodils are often our first real taste of spring. Usually one of the first flowers to bloom, the bright, cheery yellow faces of daffodils make February a lot less gloomy. Daffodils have an interesting history. They don't come from the acknowledged bulb capitol of the world, Holland. They seem to have originated in the Mediterranean areas, perhaps brought back by traders. Easy to transport, easy to grow, easy to care for, and easy to share, they have made their way around the world. If you see them in an abandoned field or wood, they are a sure sign of long ago occupants.

Around here, Narcissus usually means white flowers with a red or orange inner circle. Daffodils are usually large, single flowered yellow trumpets. Jonquils usually are smaller and sport multiple blooms per stem. Turns out, they are all technically Narcissus!

Daffodils are one of the easiest bulbs to grow. Practically disease and insect free, they are also deer and rodent proof. You can still plant them this month, if you can find the bulbs, as most places sell them in the fall. Clumps need to be divided every so often, so if yours aren't blooming like you want, try digging them up. Separate them and either replant elsewhere or share them with friends! Although they really should be left alone until the leaves die off naturally and they have finished storing energy for next year, if you have several different kinds and you want to dig up a certain kind, sometimes it's easier to dig them right after they've bloomed and you're sure just where they are!

Many things start happening about the middle of February! Valentines Day kicks it off with chocolates and flowers. Try giving someone you love a big bunch of fresh picked daffodils!

Make sure you get your Martin houses cleaned and back up as the scouts will start appearing as soon as the weather is warm enough. They are such a joy to watch, as well as being beneficial.

Time to fertilize your pecan trees so the fertilizer has a chance to get washed down before the grass starts growing and steals it all. If you haven't done a soil sample and don't know how much fertilizer to use, the following is a good rule of thumb: Two pounds per inch DBA. In English, that simply means, use two pounds of fertilizer for each inch of trunk thickness measured about five feet off the ground. (Diameter at Breast Height)

For example, if the trunk of your pecan tree is ten inches thick, measured about five feet off the ground, you would use twenty pounds of fertilizer. Spread the fertilizer evenly under the tree out to the drip-line. Using the right fertilizer makes a lot of difference. 8-8-8 or 10-10-10, with added zinc, is specially formulated for pecan trees.

Time also to spray Dormant Oil on your fruit trees, shrubs, and roses. The Dormant Oil will smother diseases and insects that have overwintered in the bark. Dormant Oil needs to be used before it hot so you won't cook your plants.

Many people start planting their cool weather crops about the middle of February. Of course, if you already planted last month and the weather co-operated, you already have a head start! Even if the weather didn't co-operate, you still have plenty of time.

# FEBRUARY

SEEDS

PLANTS

REMINDERS AND TO DO LIST

# FEBRUARY

### FERTILIZER & LIME

### PLANTING DATES

### WEATHER

### INSECTS

### HARVEST DATES

# FEBRUARY

WHAT I PLANTED WHERE

# March

    Wow! Talk about an Arctic blast! No early flowers this year! Winter advances and retreats, like expert dancers doing the Tango or some equally intricate dance. Winter is losing its grip and little by little things will turn green again.

    How encouraging to live here in the winter months instead of farther north where everything is gray and bleak. Did you ever look around at just how many plants stay green all winter? Pine trees are the most obvious, then Southern Wax Myrtles, around here known affectionately as myrkles. Hollie and camellias, nandinas and ligustrums, cedars and collards and rye grass and…

    Did you ever think about just how many shades of green there are? From the palest celadon gracing a sunset to the darkest forest edging our woods and all the colors in between, the names of the greens roll off the tongue in a joyful litany—emerald, apple, grass, jade, olive, sage, mint, moss, lime, even chartreuse.

    Make sure your houseplants are thriving—unlike them, we like the dry heat inside our homes this time of year! If the plants are small enough you can sit them in the kitchen sink and rinse them off with the spray nozzle. Remember to remove the saucer first so they don't drown. If the plants are too big to fit in the sink, but still small enough for you to move, the shower works great. If the plants are huge, simply misting them with a spray bottle will help tremendously.

    Now is a good time to check for insect pests as well. Inspect under the leaves for whiteflies, aphids, and spider mites. Whiteflies are just what they sound like—tiny white flies that live under plant leaves and fly up in a cloud when disturbed. Aphids are small and can be light green, reddish, or sometimes clear. They, too, live beneath the leaves, especially on tender new growth. Spider mites are red tiny and red and almost impossible to see. They live underneath, but a good indicator they're hiding out on your plants are leaves that have a speckled appearance on top or a plant that appears webby. Another insect to watch out for is mealybugs. These bugs look like pieces of cotton stuck in the joints.

    All these are sucking insects and can spread to other plants. If not treated, they can be fatal. Use a good insecticidal soap or insecticide that is safe for houseplants.

    Good Friday, the day when many people plant their gardens, is really early this year. March 25th to be exact! Ever wonder why

Easter can't pick a date and settle? It has everything to do with the full moon and the Vernal Equinox. The Vernal Equinox is the first day of spring, usually around the 21st of March, when the day and night are almost the same length. Easter is the first Sunday after the first full moon after the 21st of March. Make more sense now?

Theoretically, there shouldn't be any more frost after Easter. *Theoretically.*

Before you know it, red maples will be dressed in their finest, jasmine will be perfuming the air and carpeting the ground in yellow, and wisteria will be draped around and across the tops of many trees. If you notice the red maple seed pods before they helicopter off, cut a few branches. One of our local squirrels let me in on the secret—he nibbled the branches off and dropped them to the ground, seemingly just for me.

Mixed with jasmine or wisteria or by themselves, they make a beautiful and unique arrangement. The "helicopters" can also be dried and will last a long time. Some people don't like the smoky scent of wisteria, but it is a beautiful adornment to the woods.

# MARCH

SEEDS

PLANTS

REMINDERS AND TO DO LIST

# MARCH

### FERTILIZER & LIME

_____

### PLANTING DATES

_____
_____
_____
_____

### WEATHER

_____
_____
_____

### INSECTS

_____
_____

### HARVEST DATES

_____
_____
_____
_____

# MARCH

WHAT I PLANTED WHERE

# April

    April is a teenager, neither child nor adult, caught betwixt and between. By turns fractious and sullen, sunny and laughing, changing at a moment's notice with no clue which way the wind will blow. Bursting at the seams with life, everything happening at once, blink and you've missed it. A bright shining memory jewel to be taken out and treasured in the heat of summer when everything is brown and sere, a hopeful beacon in the dead of winter.

    It's time to start planting your garden in earnest. If you got it done Good Friday, here's hoping the weather is co-operating. Early April is the time to plant sweet corn so it will have time to mature before the bugs get too bad. Try some early watermelons and cantaloupes. The cold weather was supposed to be behind us with the advent of Easter, but it's almost always cold Pig Pickin' weekend. Mid April is usually good for planting warm season crops such as tomatoes, cukes, and peppers. They won't grow until the nighttime temperatures stay in the 60s or above, so getting them out too early will do more harm than good.

    If you've never been to the Azalea Festival in Wilmington, you're missing a real treat. This year's festival runs April 6-10. Wilmington warms up a week or two earlier than we do, so their azaleas start blooming before ours. Making it well worth the trip are two personal favorites, Orton Plantation and Airlie Gardens. Azaleas only bloom a couple weeks out of the year, but those weeks are more than adequate compensation for looking at their plain green shrubs the rest of the year.

    We don't enjoy the lush, fine-bladed grasses of our northern neighbors, but the grasses we have are much better suited to our climate and soil. Our grasses tend to be creeping instead of upright, light green instead of dark, thick bladed and coarse instead of soft. End of April/ first of May is usually time to fertilize, even though it's tempting to do it earlier so the grass will green up faster. Only problem with that theory is, if we get a late cold spell, as we have the last few years, it will harm the tender new growth, thus setting it back farther than if we had just been patient. A good rule of thumb is not to fertilize until after you've mowed at least once—actual grass, that is—not weeds!

    Bermuda and Centipede are two of our most popular varieties of grass. Bermuda needs more lime and fertilizer, usually 8-8-8 or 10-10-10. Bermuda will take more traffic, but has to be cut more often. Centipede doesn't like lime, but does like a a 5-5-15 with extra iron and sulphur. It won't take as much abuse, but doesn't need to be mowed nearly as often.

April is a great time for planting shrubs. Whether you're replacing a few old or winter damaged shrubs, starting a new bed, or redoing your entire landscape, now is the perfect time. Some things to consider are size and shape of the shrub, characteristics, evergreen or deciduous.

Will the mature size of the plant fit in the area you've chosen for it? If the chosen shrub gets too big, you'll spend all your time pruning and neither of you will be happy. Too small and it will always look like a child playing dress-up in an adult's clothes. If the shrub is to be placed in a high traffic area, such as beside a walk or near an entrance or exit, does it bite? If you're trying to protect Sleeping Beauty's castle, thorns are all well and good, whereas, extending a warm welcome to visitors needs a whole different plan. How does the shrub smell? Wonderfully fragrant, or like the cat's litter box? If it blooms, does it attract bees? Does the shrub stay green year round or in winter does it look like the bare bones of last year's Christmas tree? Lots of things to consider, but such fun!

It's also time to prune and fertilize most shrubs. Get rid of any dead or diseased wood, or any cold damaged branches. Most evergreens just need shaping. Some you can shear and some need to be thinned one branch at a time. Hydrangeas need the old, gray wood cut the the ground, but leave the tan or brown branches for them to bloom on. Azaleas don't need to be pruned or fertilized until after they bloom.

This is a real borderline area for Oleanders and they fared rough this winter. If they had a good root system they will probably survive. You may have to cut them back almost to the ground, but don't give up on them just yet.

Mix up some acid Miracle-Gro, the kind for Azaleas and camellias, and pour around all your shrubs, especially if they are planted around the foundation of your house. Then go back (when you fertilize your lawn is fine) and — sparingly — throw some 8-8-8 or 10-10-10 around them. They will reward you with another season of beauty.

April is a wonderful, busy month! Get out and enjoy the weather before it gets too hot. Before the flies, fleas, ticks, gnats, chiggers, mosquitoes, fire ants, snakes, and other assorted nasties drive us back inside!

# APRIL

SEEDS                            PLANTS

_____      _____
_____      _____
_____      _____
_____      _____
_____      _____
_____      _____
_____      _____
_____      _____

REMINDERS AND TO DO LIST

_____
_____
_____
_____
_____
_____
_____
_____
_____
_____
_____

# APRIL

### FERTILIZER & LIME

### PLANTING DATES

### WEATHER

### INSECTS

### HARVEST DATES

# APRIL

WHAT I PLANTED WHERE

# May

May! Ahh, May! Sweet month of May! The month when (hopefully) it's warm enough to turn the heat off and yet cool enough that we can leave the windows open for awhile and enjoy the fresh air before we have to turn on the air conditioner. May is the last tattered remnant of spring, the favored harbinger of summer. The month when our appetites change from wanting hearty soups and stews, roast with all the trimmings, and the other winter fare our bodies crave during cold weather, to wanting lighter fare such as salads, fried chicken with potato salad, anything cooked on the grill, and all the fresh fruits and vegetables we can hold.

May is the flavors of childhood; the last of the strawberries, coupled with the anticipation of the first blueberries and watermelons. That small space in time when the garden is growing in leaps and bounds and the summer weeds have just begun to remember they're first cousins to Jack's beanstalk. The month when we risk life and limb to rescue turtles crossing the road, the same turtles we'll be consigning to the depths of Hades next month when when they're helping themselves to our cantaloupes and tomatoes. Hopefully, you're beginning to harvest some of the early crops such as peas and cabbage, although this year's unusual cold has thrown everything off schedule. Mid to end of May is time to plant butter beans, okra, sweet potatoes, field peas, and peanuts. These crops love warm nights and won't grow until the nighttime temps stay in the 60s.

Along with the warm temps and good growing conditions come the insect pests. Make sure you keep an eye out for them, as they multiply exponentially and can wreak havoc seemingly overnight. Most insects hatch out worse around a full moon, so be extra vigilant then.

Lantana—one of our favorite, easy to grow flowers. Most times in our area they are perennial, but they don't like cold weather. If yours haven't come back yet, don't despair and pitch them just yet. Give them until at least the end of May before giving something else their spot. The last few years lantana have been bothered by lantana lace bugs. If your leaves—once they do come back—turn kind of brown and curly, you probably have lace bugs. Spray with a good systemic insecticide early and head them off.

May is also a great time to spray crape myrtles to head off the aphids that love to feast on all the new growth. This, combined with a good systemic fungicide, will also help ward off the sooty mildew on your crapes. Systemic means the chemical gets into the plant and will stay effective longer than a spray that just coats the leaves and will only last a short time.

Confused about whether to plant annuals or perennials? What's the difference? Annual means it has to be planted every year, perennial means the plant will return all by itself, year after year. Some good examples of annuals are marigolds, petunias, salvias, impatiens, and portulaca. Perennials can be anything from roses to iris to phlox and peonies.

Annuals have been bred to give us lots of color all summer, while most perennials, at least here, bloom for a short time and then go dormant until next year. For season long blooms, mix annuals and perennials for a true show stopping display.

Your flowerbeds should please you, so whether you like a one or two color scheme, such as red and white, or whether you like a hodgepodge of every color known to man is a matter of individual taste. While you're having fun, think out of the box! Flowerbeds don't have to just be flat, they can also be vertical!

Using a trellis or fence, extend your garden up with colorful and interesting vines such as perennial clematis, annuals like black-eyed Susan vine or cypress vine, or even edible ornamentals such as hyacinth bean or Malabar spinach.

Don't have time or room for elaborate beds? Try container gardening! A single red geranium in a planter can really dress up your porch or walkway. Want something more attention grabbing? Try an eye-popping mixture such as purple setcreasea (Moses in a boat) mixed with some lime green ornamental sweet potato vine and hot pink wave petunias!

Roses are a popular Mother's Day gift. Whether you give one or get one, they need some special care. Roses are extremely susceptible to black spot, which is just what it sounds like. If not properly sprayed about once a week to every ten days, the leaves will develop black spots surrounded by yellowing patches. The roses will shed off these leaves in an effort to save itself.

Eventually, you will end up with a naked plant that has no way to produce food. The rose basically starves to death. There aren't any cures for black spot, only preventatives. Some things you can do to help include proper and timely spraying, and keeping the plant healthy by fertilizing and pruning. Use a good systemic fungicide and start spraying as soon as the roses leaf out and the weather starts to stay warm at night.

When you water, don't splash water on the leaves as this can spread the black spot spores. If you find any contaminated leaves, pick them off and get rid of them—burn them or put them in the trashcan. Roses are heavy feeders, so give them plenty of fertilizer. They also like Epsom salt, about one tablespoon to a gallon of water, poured around the plant.

While you're pruning, don't forget to cut a big bouquet and enjoy!

# MAY

SEEDS

PLANTS

REMINDERS AND TO DO LIST

# MAY

### FERTILIZER & LIME

### PLANTING DATES

### WEATHER

### INSECTS

### HARVEST DATES

# MAY

WHAT I PLANTED WHERE

# JUNE

June is like a stroll down the beach; beautiful, but the longer you walk, the hotter it gets.

June is graduations and weddings, summer camp and Bible school, family reunions and cookouts punctuated by the shouts of "school's out" and followed closely by the predictable refrain of "I'm bored."

Crape myrtles and hydrangeas are in full bloom and the heady scent of gardenias fills the air. Lightning bugs are blinking out the insect version of Morse code, calling to children of all ages, "catch me if you can!"

Everyone is anticipating the first ripe tomatoes and the first of the sweet corn. Fresh bread, a sprinkle of salt, some bacon, some mayonnaise, a bit of lettuce and some butter equals a meal fit for a king!

March, like a scratched record, stuttered and repeated itself, then completely skipped April and most of May. On the other hand, do you ever remember the azaleas lasting as long as they have this year? Even our recent nor'easter didn't dim their beauty much. Due to the fact that most of our gardens have been turned into duck impoundments, don't suppose there will be much in the way of early crops, but the cool season crops such as lettuce have done extremely well this year.

Mid June to mid July is usually time to plant a second crop of tomatoes, but this year it may be the earliest planting that survives! Mid June is also time to plant pumpkins. If you plant pumpkins in March or early April, you'll have pumpkins for the 4th of July!

Should your butterbeans and peanuts ever get big enough to start blooming, it's time to dust them with land plaster. This helps them fill out. You can also dust tomatoes with land plaster, as it is a form of calcium and will help prevent blossom end rot.

Blossom end rot is the disease that makes a rotten spot on the bottom of an otherwise perfectly beautiful tomato. Lots of things can cause blossom end rot. Too much water, too little water, cool nights, the list goes on and on. Basically, it's just a lack of calcium. Sometimes the plant will self correct. Putting lime in the hole when planting will help. You can also use a calcium spray when the plants start blooming. Besides, the calcium is about the only thing you have any control over.

If you move your houseplants outside for the summer, now is a good time to replant. Plants, like people, can outgrow their living space. As a general rule, plants should be moved up about one pot size. Otherwise, it's like a toddler wearing daddy's boots. Keep in mind, don't expose them to too much sunlight at first, as they can also get sunburned.

Whatever type of container you choose, remember that if there are no drainage holes in the bottom of it, you don't have a planter, you have a water garden and unless you have aquatic plants, your plants will drown.

Plastic and clay pots both have advantages and disadvantages. Plastic is more durable than clay, so if it gets knocked over or dropped, it's not as likely to break, although sunlight will eventually make plastic brittle. Clay is more breakable, but friendlier to plants. Plastic won't discolor like clay when the salts from water and fertilizer leach out of your soil. If you use clay pots, when they become discolored, remove the plants and, depending on how badly they're discolored, either spray or soak the pots in a mild solution of vinegar, then clean gently with a plastic scrubbie or soft cloth.

The growing medium is very important too. Whether you choose potting soil, which is actual dirt, or potting medium, which is a manmade mixture of peat, bark, ash, charcoal, vermiculite, and perlite, is up to you. Some plants like heavier soils and some prefer a lighter mixture that drains better. Some plants, like spider plants and aloe, like to be root bound. They won't reproduce unless they are root bound.

While you're transplanting, don't forget about feeding your plants. Many types of plant food are available. You can use a time release product, such as Osmocote. You've seen them, those little green or gold balls you see in lots of plants and shrubs. Osmocote is released by heat and will usually last about three months. This way, if you forget to fertilize, they still get some nourishment.

Water soluble means a product such as Miracle-Gro, a powder that you mix with water.

Fertilize regularly and your plants will reward you by growing vigorously and staying green and beautiful. Once a week is good, more often if it rains a lot or you water often.

Don't fertilize when plants are wilted and don't let them dry out to the point of wilting for a day or two after you fertilize. This can cause tip burn on the leaves.

If your petunias or geraniums start yellowing and fertilizing doesn't help, they could be iron deficient. Iron is available in both liquid and granular forms. The granular form can stain concrete, so be careful if you spill any on sidewalks, etc. Just sweep it up before it gets wet.

Keep your squash and cucumbers dusted for squash vine borers, especially around the base of the stem. A nocturnal moth flies by, drills a hole and deposits some eggs. The eggs hatch and eat all the pith inside the stem. About the time your squash start bearing, the plant keels over because it has no way to feed itself.

Enjoy your garden and your gardening—before everything starts coming off at once and you can't eat nor can fast enough!

# JUNE

SEEDS

PLANTS

REMINDERS AND TO DO LIST

# JUNE

### FERTILIZER & LIME

### PLANTING DATES

### WEATHER

### INSECTS

### HARVEST DATES

# JUNE

## WHAT I PLANTED WHERE

# JULY

Rain, rain, go away! Whatever happened to gentle showers? We seem to have been relegated to the downpour and deluge section! Let's hope the summer isn't as wet as the spring. Good thing we have plenty of grocery stores.

It's July and the fun of planting things and watching them grow wanes a little more with each rise in temperature. The work begins in earnest as crops start coming off, each needing to be canned, or pickled, or frozen, or just plain eaten. In between picking and preparing, the never ending task of weeding rears its ugly head, again and again and again, until every time we close our eyes, all we see is weeds. The morning chatter of song birds has given way to the buzzing drone of cicadas, reminding us over and over, as if we hadn't noticed, or had somehow managed to forget, "Hot, it's hot."

Speaking of weeds—what is a weed? A simple definition of a weed is any plant that is growing where you don't want it. All plants are weeds somewhere! If you spray your garden with weed killer, not only will you kill what we consider to be weeds, you will also kill all your vegetables. Why? Because weed killers don't distinguish between weeds you want and weeds you don't. Weed killers are designed to kill either broadleaf weeds or grass, or a combination of the two. Broadleaf weeds are plants that have veins that spread out like your hand. Grassy type weeds are weeds with veins that run up and down like stripes. This difference is what allows you to spray your yard to get rid of broadleaf weeds without killing your grass, and farmers to spray their crops to kill grass without harming their crops. Some chemicals, like Roundup, kill everything. Spreader sticker can be added to weed killers to help them work. Spreader sticker makes the chemicals stick to the weed leaves better. Some weeds are harder to kill than others and require repeated sprayings. Gardening would be so much easier if we let the weeds grow and killed the vegetables! July is time to spray poison ivy. The leaves have to be mature for weed killers to work on it.

If you planted chrysanthemums last fall and they've come back, they will probably start blooming sometime around the end of July. If you want really bushy plants that are full of blooms for fall, about the middle of the month you need to cut them back to about six or eight inches tall. It's hard to do when they are just starting to bloom, but they come up too early here, so they bloom too early, and by fall, when we need some color, they are spent. Don't forget to fertilize after you cut them back!

Try planting some late tomatoes, peppers, cukes and squash, maybe a late crop of green beans. Just remember to keep them dusted or sprayed. Insect pests are out in full force and they are ravenous! Winter keeping squash, such as butternut, should be planted now so that they will come off late in the fall. As late as we've been having our first frost, tomatoes planted now should bear well into the fall.

If you seed your own collards and cabbage for fall planting, mid July is the time to start. Normally, they can be transplanted in about four to five weeks or so, depending on the weather. Don't forget to keep them dusted or sprayed and watered.

As much rain as we've had, you wouldn't think we'd ever have to water again. Things tend to dry out rapidly in our heat, though. Plants can't get up and move to a cooler spot, so they wilt in order to decrease leaf surface and to conserve moisture. Plants exhibit the same symptoms for too much water as they do for not enough water. If your plants are wilting and watering isn't helping, check to make sure they aren't too wet and that they have adequate drainage, especially potted plants. With all the rain, the roots can easily get rotted off so that the plant wilts and droops, just as if it needs water. When you see a plant wilting, your first response is to water it more. This only compounds the problem and by the time you realize it's had too much water, it's usually too late. If this turns out to be the case, ease off watering for a couple of days and keep a close eye on the plant. Try not to water again until the soil has had a chance to dry out some. Maybe it's not too late! Try to water in the morning, as this gives the plants most of the day to dry off and really helps cut down on fungus and bacteria. It's better to soak gardens and lawns every other day than to spritz them every day. A general rule is to water until the soil is wet about an inch deep. Hanging baskets and potted plants need water at least once a day, and sometimes twice.

Don't forget about deadheading. Deadheading is removing the spent blooms or too large vegetables from your plants. Plants don't produce flowers or veggies for our benefit. They produce them so that there will be seed for next year. If there are lots of dead blooms, or lots of over-ripe veggies, then the plant thinks it has done its job and may quit producing. If you keep the flowers and veggies picked, then the plant is fooled into making more in order to insure next year's crop of seeds. Deadheading is also a time honored way to save seeds. Keep in mind that if your plants are hybrids, saving seeds won't do you much good, because the seeds will revert to one of the parents, and probably won't be what you wanted.

# JULY

SEEDS

PLANTS

REMINDERS AND TO DO LIST

# JULY

### FERTILIZER & LIME

### PLANTING DATES

### WEATHER

### INSECTS

### HARVEST DATES

# JULY

WHAT I PLANTED WHERE

# August

August is the highest hill on the rollercoaster ride of the seasons. After chug-chug-chugging to the very top, that breathless moment just before the plunge is going to be bad, but there's no backing out now. The only thing you can do is take a deep breath, hold on tight, and hope you make it to the end of the ride.

Heat that just keeps building and building until you wonder if it will ever be cool again. Road snakes shimmer across the highway, making you wonder if you actually did see something or if the heat really has made you crazy. Having no appetite for anything but fruit salads and frozen confections. August is being wrapped in a wet wool blanket and trapped in a sauna on stuck on high.

August is all about just hanging on.

The weatherman might as well go on vacation for the month of August because we all know the forecast by heart. Hot, hazy, and humid with a chance of afternoon thunderboomers. Everything—plant, animal, and human—is hunkered down in the coolest available spot trying to survive until the weather cools off. The only variation in the weather theme is the threat of a hurricane.

Plants can't evacuate during a hurricane so we have to do what we can to help them. Move potted plants inside or at least to a sheltered location. Larger shrubs and trees are pretty much on their own, at least until after the storm. If we get a salt storm, the kind where we just get the salt spray blown in off the ocean, without lots of rain afterward, rinsing shrubs and trees with fresh water as soon as possible will minimize damage.

Some plants are salt tolerant, which is why they can survive on the beach. Most are not, and salt spray will burn their leaves off. Plants aren't—and shouldn't be—our first priority, but they do deserve some consideration, especially as much money as some of us spend on our plants!

Rake up dead leaves and branches, prune out damaged sections, and check for insect pests. Plants, just like people, are more susceptible to diseases and other problems when they are stressed, and hurricanes are high on the stress scale.

Fire ants love to invade potted plants, especially when the surrounding land is flooded and they are looking for higher ground. Fire ants are like icebergs. The nest you see above ground is only a small portion of the whole mound. Fire ant nests go down—in some cases ten feet or more—looking for coolness and moisture. That's why after a hurricane, it seems as if all these huge mounds pop up overnight. When the ground becomes saturated, they build *up* in an effort to stay dry. Fire ant killers are in high demand after hurricanes, so you might want to stock up ahead of time!

If you see wasps flying around your shrubs, before reaching for the wasp spray—carefully!—check your shrubs to see if mealy bugs are trying to take over. Mealy bugs are cottony looking growths, usually located in the forks of the branches. They secrete a sweet, sticky substance that the wasps like. Mealy bugs can eventually kill a plant, so the wasps are actually doing us a favor by acting as an early warning system.

Seems like everything is out to kill tomatoes! If the plants survive, blossom end rot and insects take a big toll. Merely getting the plants to survive anymore is a miracle in itself. We all know about regular (fusarium) wilt. One day your tomato plant is big, beautiful, healthy, and full of tomatoes. The next day, it looks like someone poured boiling water on the plant and it's history. There's no known cure, except cold weather, cold enough to freeze the ground several inches deep, because fusarium is a fungus that lives in the soil. Keeping your garden tilled in the winter can help, especially if we have cold winters like the past few.

That, or planting in containers and using a good, sterilized potting soil. Fusarium wilt enters the plant through the roots so anything that damages the roots can make it worse. Such as, too much rain rotting off feeder roots, soil nematodes, and hoeing too close.

The last few years, tomato spotted wilt virus has taken over. The plants get up a foot or two, and everything looks great. First you notice a little bronzing on the top leaves. Then the leaves start curling under and the plant becomes stunted. If the plant makes it long enough to produce, the tomatoes are small and often discolored, with yellow spots or mottling. This disease is caused by a tiny insect called a thrip.

The thrip carries the disease, kind of like mosquitoes and malaria. Once he bites the plant, it's toast. Pull it up and get rid of it. Burn it or bag it, but do not put it in your compost pile. This nasty little bug can be blown in on the wind or it can live in tall grass and weeds around your garden. No cure for this one either. Somebody better come up with something quick or summer's most beloved vegetable is going to go the way of the dinosaurs. This disease also affects peppers, peanuts, eggplant, tobacco...

Plants suffer as much from the heat as people. Flower blooms get smaller and fewer, vegetable plants wind down, producing less and less until they finally give up altogether. Some flowers can be pruned back so when it does cool off, they will get a new flush of growth and delight you until frost.

Vegetables can be replanted for late crops. If you can stand the heat, August is not too late to plant another crop of green beans, cukes—be sure to keep them dusted for pickle worms—okra, and a few other short term veggies.

Keep them watered!

End of August is time to start thinking about beginning to plant cole crops such as collards, cabbage, turnips, and rutabagas. Wait a couple more weeks, depending on the heat, to plant things like broccoli and lettuce. They are more susceptible to heat and will bolt—go to seed—fast.

# AUGUST

SEEDS

PLANTS

REMINDERS AND TO DO LIST

# AUGUST

### FERTILIZER & LIME

_____

### PLANTING DATES

_____
_____
_____
_____

### WEATHER

_____
_____
_____

### INSECTS

_____
_____

### HARVEST DATES

_____
_____
_____
_____

# AUGUST

WHAT I PLANTED WHERE

# September

September is here! Although it won't be much cooler for awhile, the hottest days, the dog days of summer, are behind us. Perhaps they are called dog days because they make us all as crazy as a rabid dog! However, with the slightest hint...promise... hope...intimation...even the merest thought of cooler weather, our spirits are rising as well as our energy levels. Tempers. like thermometers, are slowly falling back into more acceptable ranges.

The big yellow, delightfully annoying munchkin conveyances are out in full force, like huge mobile dandelions. With each open and shut of their doors, like a child blowing on a dandelion puff, they scatter children every which way as if they were windblown seeds.

The sun, having been a fierce enemy for the last couple of months, has become an almost friend again. Our appetites are still geared for hot weather, but we'll catch ourselves dropping a bag of dried baby limas in the shopping cart this week, next week fixings for chili—just in case!

Summer flowers are giving way to fall mums, and our color schemes are changing, mimicking nature.

After a well deserved hiatus, the gardening world is cranking back up. September is time to plant cole crops for fall. Collards, cabbage, broccoli, spinach, chard, lettuce, and Brussels sprouts should be available at your local nurseries. Collards and cabbage should be available from the first of the month onward. Broccoli, lettuce, spinach, Brussels sprouts, and chard like a little cooler weather so they may not be quite ready to plant until later in the month. These plants will bolt quickly in hot weather, so it's best to start them a little later.

Time to plant seeds for turnips and rutabagas, as well as mixed salad or other greens such as kale or mustard. Onion sets should be available about the middle of September. If you can finds some fall vidalia plants they will do well also.

Ever notice how some people have a wonderfully green lawn all winter? Wish you could? It's simple! If you want a lush green lawn all winter, mid September is time to over-seed with winter rye grass. Five to ten pounds per thousand square feet should do the trick nicely. Add a little fertilizer, and voila! Keep in mind, if you have a lush green lawn, someone has to mow that aforementioned lush green lawn all winter. Annual rye has to be planted every year, but on the other hand, it dies out in late spring, when the weather gets hot.

Now is also time to plant clover, whether you plant it as a cover crop for your garden or you just like to see it bloom in the spring.

There's still time to plant some herbs so you'll have some fresh ones all winter. If you're doing them from seed, most will come up in around a week. Keep in mind that parsley can take a month or so to germinate, so if you don't see results right away, don't give up! Keep the soil moist and have patience! Whether you do them in individual pots of a single mixed pot of your favorites depends only on the width of your windowsill! Herb plants can also be found at some nurseries. Just think how good that fresh sage or thyme is going to taste with the Thanksgiving turkey and stuffing!

While we're thinking ahead, it's time to start bulbs if you want to force them for Christmas. Forcing bulbs means fooling the plant into blooming ahead of its natural schedule. Forcing bulbs is easy, it just requires a little time and planning. First, choose bulbs that are suitable for forcing. These include, but aren't limited to: crocuses, daffodils, hyacinths, and tulips. Most catalogs will note the right ones for forcing.

The pot needs to be at least twice as tall as the bulbs. Fill the pot half full with good potting soil, or until the points of the bulbs almost reach the top of the pot. Fill the rest of the way, covering the bulbs. It's fine if the tips of the bulbs are showing. Don't forget to make sure you have good drainage! Moisten thoroughly and place in a cool, dark spot. Since it doesn't usually get cold enough to chill these outside here, the refrigerator makes a great substitute. Bulbs must be chilled for 12-16 weeks, or until you see shoots two to three inches tall and roots coming out the bottom of the pot. Bulbs can be potted up anytime from mid September to late December, depending on when you want them to bloom.

In general, mid September plantings will flower around mid to late December. For blooms in February, plant in mid October; for March, plant in mid November. Some general rules to follow: the smaller the bulb, the more you can put in a pot. Pointed ends usually go up. Bulbs should be close but not touching. Keep them moist.

When you first take them out of the frig, put them in a cool room with indirect light. After they green up, they can be moved to a warmer, sunnier room. Depending on what type of bulb and the room temperature, they can last anywhere from several days to a couple of weeks.

Bulbs that can be forced without chilling are narcissus (paperwhites) and amaryllis. Instead of soil, the narcissus can be put in a pot full of pebbles or gravel, no drainage required for this one. Fill the pot with water to just below the the top of the pebbles. Keep them in low light for two to three weeks, keeping the water level constant until shoots appear and the bulbs are well rooted. Remember that narcissus have an intense fragrance, so a few of these will go a long way! Hyacinths are extremely fragrant as well.

Amaryllis can be forced in four to six weeks. They need to be started in a warm, well lit place (in soil) although once they start blooming, the blooms will last longer if they're kept in a cooler room. These pots of forced bulbs are great for cheering yourself up in the winter time and they also make wonderful gifts.

When they are done blooming, all but the paperwhites can be planted out in your flowerbed to be enjoyed another year. Let them stay in the pots until the foliage dies back, then plant them in your flowerbed. Make sure you give them a little extra fertilizer when you do. Forcing them to bloom stresses them, so they may not bloom a whole lot the following year.

# SEPTEMBER

SEEDS

PLANTS

REMINDERS AND TO DO LIST

# SEPTEMBER

## FERTILIZER & LIME

## PLANTING DATES

## WEATHER

## INSECTS

## HARVEST DATES

# SEPTEMBER

## WHAT I PLANTED WHERE

# October

October is here! If not our most beautiful month, surely it must be tied for first. The sky is a perfect azure dome, making us feel like living inhabitants of a world size snow globe. The temperatures are perfect, energizing everyone. Cool at night, just right during the day.

All that yard work we've been putting off all summer is calling to us, and we're actually listening again. Those of us unfortunate to have to work all day and fortunate enough to own slow cookers and bread machines will be pulling them out and getting up a little earlier. The loss of a bit of sleep will be more than worth coming home to a big pot of beef stew or chili or a nice roast with veggies, along with a loaf of hot bread ready to welcome us home. Besides, if supper's already cooked, that gives us more time to work in the yard!

Fall is such an exciting time of year! Spider webs, invisible all summer, appear each morning as if by magic. From the tiniest ones hung between blades of grass to the huge ones strung high up between trees and power lines, the dew clings to them making them look like they're woven out of strands of sparkling jewels.

The leaves are changing color and drifting down. Soon the wind will be blowing them across the road, skittering on their dried points as if they were hordes of demented rodents bent on getting to the other side.

Mums are in full bloom. Don't forget the Mum Festival at Tryon Palace. The date this year is October 8th and 9th. This year marks the 25th anniversary for the Mum Fest so it should be extra special.

Chrysanthemums come in lots of colors, the most popular being yellow, but also include white, red, purple, pumpkin color, pink, even bi-colors. There are also different types of blooms on mums. Decorative seems to be the most common, but you can get anemone, daisy, spider, spoon-tipped, and quilled. Different mum varieties bloom at different times, so with a little careful planning, you can make them last a good while. Most varieties can be planted outside here and will come back next year. Keep in mind that they come up too early here and need to be whacked back to about eight inches sometime around the middle of July—Fourth of July is a great reminder!—if you want them to bloom in the fall.

October is time to start planting ornamental cabbage and kale. Treat the ornamental cabbage and kale just as you would regular cole crops. Keep them dusted or sprayed for worms and insects. Cold weather enhances their beauty, brings out the colors, helps them keep a nice uniform shape, and keeps them from bolting. These plants are really cold dependent and too much warm weather makes them go kaput. On the other hand, the birds really like the seeds and the yellow flowers are kind of pretty.

    Time for pansies! Pansies are our longest blooming annual. They bloom from October until the end of May or so, depending on when the weather gets too hot for them. Pansies, too, come in a variety of sizes and colors. Some pansies have blotches, or faces, while some are solid colors. Purple, black, yellow, orange, white, mixes, bi-colors, tri-colors, and lots of shades in between. Some of the new color developments are truly astonishing. From giant pansies with huge blooms to tiny violas, as well as mid-size pansies, the choices are numerous. Pansies are beautiful by themselves or mixed with snapdragons, curly parsley, or lettuces. Try mixing them with the ornamental cabbage and kale!

    If you haven't already, it's time to dig sweet potatoes! They need to cure for several weeks after being dug to reach their full flavor potential. Once dug and cured, they can be stored in a cool, dry place. Anywhere cool that won't freeze is will work. If you don't have anywhere like that to store them, try baking a bunch of them and putting them in the freezer. Simply bake them, let them cool, then you can slip the skins off (or not), put them in a Ziplock freezer bag or freezer container, and they'll be ready when you need them. Especially nice when unexpected dinner guests show up! Whether you prefer the small, one person size sweet potato or the huge one-potato-makes-a-pie size, enjoy them.

    Sweet potatoes are really good for you, as well as being delicious. There are oodles of sweet potato recipes floating around and everyone has a favorite. French fried sweet potatoes, sweet potato soufflé, sweet potato pie, sweet potato bread, sweet potato biscuits, or a plain baked sweet potato with a little butter and salt or maybe brown sugar and cinnamon. You get the picture!

    If you put your houseplants outside for the summer, don't forget to bring them back in before it freezes. Also, if you didn't change the soil they're in when you put them out in the spring, you probably need to do it now while they're still outside. Do any necessary pruning or dividing outside as well and save yourself from making a big mess in the house. Check the plants and pots for creepy-crawlies and spray if needed. You definitely don't want to bring any bugs in with your plants!

If you got motivated last month and started some bulb pots in the frig, don't forget to keep an eye on them.

Early October is getting late, but not too late to plant cole crops. And yes, it's cole, not cold! Cole crops means any plants in the cabbage family suitable for growing in cold weather. Cabbage, broccoli, cauliflower, Brussels sprouts, collards, mustard greens, etc. You can still plant them, they just won't have as much time to grow.

There are tons of fall grasses and seed pods that will make wonderful and unusual flower arrangements. Spray them with hairspray before taking them inside. This will help set them so don't continue opening and shed seeds all over, as well as killing any bugs that are hitching a ride. A few other things to keep in mind: If the plants aren't on your property ask permission first, watch out for bugs and snakes, don't harvest anything on the endangered list (think Sea Oats), and remember hunting seasons. Watch out for poison ivy; its leaves turn beautiful shades of red. Make sure you know what it looks like before you go leaf gathering! Leaves of three, leave it be!

Gather up some pumpkins, mums, cornstalks, maybe some unusual leaves and enjoy decorating for this month!

# OCTOBER

SEEDS

PLANTS

REMINDERS AND TO DO LIST

# OCTOBER

### FERTILIZER & LIME

### PLANTING DATES

### WEATHER

### INSECTS

### HARVEST DATES

# OCTOBER

WHAT I PLANTED WHERE

# November

November is a month of wonder!

Wondering whether to wear shorts or jeans, tank tops or jackets.

Wondering where the summer went, and how did the holiday season arrive so fast—wasn't it here just a few short weeks ago?

Wondering whether, after a long season of shorts and flip flops, we can still fit into last year's jeans?

Wondering where, exactly, in the closet did we put our favorite sweater?

Wondering where all the leaves came from and what in the world am I going to do with all of them?

A month for mullet blows and the first oyster roasts, with a huge pot of clam chowder and a pan of cornbread as sides.

Can't help you with the answers to the first questions, but as for the leaves… You can either rake them into big piles and burn them, or bag them and send them to the landfill. A third option, composting, may be the answer you've been looking for. While the smell of leaves burning in the fall is an integral part of childhood memories, many places don't allow burning anymore. Sending them to the landfill creates its own problems. Some statistics say as much as thirty percent or the material taken to landfills consists of yard waste.

Composting is nature's way of making more soil. Compost is the decomposed remains of once living material that becomes rich, crumbly soil. A compost pile can be as simple as a pile in the corner of your year. If you want to get a little more high-tech, a piece of chicken wire or stock wire bent in a circle and standing on end will help keep your pile contained. If you want really high-tech, you can spend a lot of money on any of a variety of the latest technology in composters. They all do the same thing.

Composting is a simple process that requires minimal maintenance. Compost piles need food, air, and water. Food can be grass clippings, leaves, wood chips, manure, and things from your kitchen such as potato peels, fruit peels, coffee grounds, and egg shells. Remember not to put diseased plants on your compost pile as many diseases can carry over from year to year. Meat scraps or cooked food can attract unwanted animals such as raccoons and possums. Watch out for fire ants as well. If they start thinking your compost pile is the perfect beach front condo, discourage them by sprinkling some hydrated lime over the pile—it burns their little feetsies off.

Two kinds of bacteria help breakdown yard waste into soil. The good kind, aerobic, needs air to work. If you want to get a jump start, there are products on the market that contain good bacteria to help you. The bad kind, anaerobic, doesn't need air. They're what makes your compost pile smell like rotting garbage. Grass clippings and leaves tend to mat. If they get too wet, they get slimy and produce anaerobic bacteria. This is why air is so crucial to composting. Your pile needs to be turned over in some way on a regular basis, either with a pitchfork or shovel. Some of the composters are actually set up to tumble, relieving you of some of the work.

Moisture is also important. Not enough water causes the good bacteria to die. Too much water causes the bad bacteria to proliferate.

A good compost pile encourages earthworms, which in turn helps the compost stay aerated as well as enriching the soil. Compost benefits the soil in several ways. In our sandy soil, it not only adds organic material, it helps hold water and returns vital nutrients to the soil. When ready, compost smells like freshly plowed earth.

Compost can be used in several different ways. It can be added directly to the soil, used as mulch, or you can make compost tea. Compost tea is made by simply combining equal parts of compost and water and letting it steep for a bit before pouring the liquid around your plants.

Speaking of earthworms, remember when you were little and you could go out and turn over anything in the yard and find enough worms to fish all afternoon? For whatever reason, there aren't many earthworms anymore. Whether it's too much fertilizers and pesticides, or the climate has changed, who can say? Earthworms are like aerobic bacteria—they need just the right conditions to thrive. Worms tunnel through the soil, aerating and creating space for plant roots. Their manure, called castings, enriches the soul. Just like frogs and green snakes, their presence is an important indicator of the health of the land.

It's still a little early to plant bulbs here. It simply doesn't get cold enough anymore to plant the bulbs in the fall. If you find some you like, go ahead and buy them because they'll probably be long gone by the time you're ready to plant. Simply store them in the frig or freezer until you're ready to plant. As wet as this summer has been, you're better off waiting anyway. The bulbs are just as likely to rot if planted now.

One of the hardier, old fashioned, exquisitely delightful bulbs that grow well in our area with little or no care, is lycoris radiata. Known better by its common names, spider lily or surprise lily, it usually blooms in late fall. One day there's nothing. Suddenly a tall shoot appears, then, like magic, a poof of bright red flowers! They also come in pink or white. The leaves come up after the plant blooms. Lycoris are especially striking planted in masses or along fence lines. Another wonder for November: wondering when they'll bloom There were a few blooming about mid October this year. They don't necessarily bloom every year, so enjoy them when they do. These are a great pass along plant.

Some of your bulbs that you put in the frig for forced blooming may be getting close to being ready to take out near the end of November. Don't forget to keep an eye on them.

It's a pretty safe bet that with all the wet weather we've had, fall gardens probably won't do much better than our summer ones. Here's hoping at least some of yours survived the flood!

# NOVEMBER

SEEDS

PLANTS

REMINDERS AND TO DO LIST

# NOVEMBER

### FERTILIZER & LIME

_____

### PLANTING DATES

_____
_____
_____
_____

### WEATHER

_____
_____
_____

### INSECTS

_____
_____

### HARVEST DATES

_____
_____
_____
_____

# NOVEMBER

## WHAT I PLANTED WHERE

# December

Think there's not much going on in the gardening world this time of year?

Think again!

Outdoors, even though many plants have lost their leaves, many others are just beginning to shine. The red berries or holly, yaupon, pyracantha, and nandina put on a pretty show as well as being food for our feathered friends. Camellias, with their cheery blossoms of red, pink, white, or sometimes even variegated red or pink, show off when hardly anything else is blooming.

Inside it's time for Christmas cactus, poinsettias, and Christmas trees. Christmas cactus come in a variety of colors, including red, salmon, pink, white, and violet. Christmas cactus can be long lived with proper care. They like to be evenly moist, which means don't let them dry out and don't over water. Christmas cactus need more potash, so when fertilizing use a water soluble such as Miracle-Gro for tomatoes. Keep them away from drafts and vents, and if possible try to keep them in a north or east window. In late spring, after danger of frost has passed, put them out in a shady place and they will reward you with beautiful blooms again next year.

Poinsettias come in many colors besides the standard red, and new colors are being introduced every year. Water as needed, but don't let water stand in the saucer. When poinsettias are done blooming, most people throw them out. With a little care they can be kept year to year. Trim back to about six inches and after danger of frost, put them outside. Move them up to a planter two to four inches larger than the one they are in. Remember to turn them so they don't become one-sided and pinch for a fuller plant. About September, bring them in and keep them in the dark for twelve to fifteen hours a day. Water sparingly until color starts to show. When the leaves are mostly colored up, bring them back out and enjoy!

Live Christmas trees smell so wonderful! Be careful not to let them dry out, as this will cause them to drop needles rapidly, as well as becoming a fire hazard. Try to keep them away from vents and other heat sources.

Now is a good time to prune roses. It's usually cold enough by now that they won't try to leaf back out until spring. Keep in mind that climbing roses bloom on old wood, so if you prune them much they won't bloom next year. Climbers should only be pruned if the canes are dead, diseased, or in your way. Bush type roses bloom on new growth, so they should be pruned back to about 18 inches. Shrub roses and rugosas generally only need to be pruned every couple of years.

Rose hips are the reddish orange berries you see on some roses. Rose hips are good food for wildlife as well as being decorative inside or out, so if you have rose hips, you may want to wait to prune your roses.

If at all possible, keep your garden tilled. We don't get much cold around here but if you can keep your garden soil turned over, especially during a cold snap, it will help kill some of the insects and diseases and possibly, some of the weed seeds.

Enjoy your winter plants, inside and out, and have a Merry Christmas!

# DECEMBER

SEEDS

PLANTS

REMINDERS AND TO DO LIST

# DECEMBER

### FERTILIZER & LIME

### PLANTING DATES

### WEATHER

### INSECTS

### HARVEST DATES

# DECEMBER

WHAT I PLANTED WHERE

An enthusiastic reader as well as author, I wrote the gardening article for The Newport Voice for many years, and thoroughly enjoyed it! I've worked at Newport Garden Center for…more years than I care to admit. I love gardening, and sharing gardening knowledge. Please don't take my ramblings as Gospel! If your gardening methods work for you, then by all means, keep doing what you're doing! Gardening is as individual as each of us, and I'm all about whatever works. Gardeners love to share ideas and how to's and plants and seeds. I hope you enjoy my articles and journal pages.

If you're looking for something else to read… I also write fiction. Adult under H S Skinner, and Young Adult/ teen under Heidi Skinner.

Made in the USA
Columbia, SC
19 February 2022